a relational [video] grammar: extrapolation

Kate Pelling

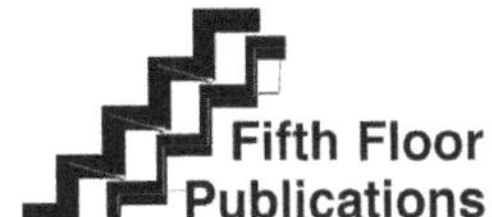

a relational [video] grammar: extrapolation
By Kate Pelling
Published by Fifth Floor Publications, London 2013

ISBN 978-0-9576128-0-8

Introduction

In the last few years I have been obsessed with editing processes, and particularly the combination of editing processes that take place during the making of direct address to camera within a context of artists' film and video. My obsession has resulted in a practice-led body of work, titled *a relational video grammar*, that is concerned with the conceptual relationship between the linguistic self-editing that occurs when an individual speaks directly to the camera, and the technological editing processes that follow the recording of that speech. This publication is part of this body of work, and it is the consequence of an important step forward in my thinking on the subject of editing direct address to camera: that the medium of video is not the only method of examining direct address to camera, nor necessarily the ultimate result of the process.

a relational [video] grammar: extrapolation is an editing experiment that uses drawing and the addition/reconfiguration/obliteration of text, to test the conceptual relationship between linguistic and technological editing processes. The publication has been produced alongside, but independently of, a series of experimental videos. These videos used a variety of techniques to explore the direct address to camera made by six individual participants. Using participants other than myself in these videos has allowed me to examine the process of direct address to camera under conditions that extend beyond my own experience. For the recording of each of the videos within this series, the participant was invited to talk directly to the camera for 30 minutes. There was no script, no words prepared in advance. They were left alone with the camera. A timer was on hand to let them know how long they had left. Following the recording, I edited the video material that had been generated, with the aim of using editing processes as a tool for understanding the relationships between the participant, the generation of speech, the edited video and the editor. The related videos are (in alphabetical order):

a relational video grammar: affective editor (2012, video, 8:47 mins.) featuring Otelo M Fabião
a relational video grammar: disavowal (2012, video, 10:18 mins.) featuring Tzvet Lazar
a relational video grammar: grammas grammat (2013, video, 7:53 mins.) featuring Michael Twaits
a relational video grammar: orange obverse (2012, video, 6:41 mins.) featuring James Graham-Campbell
a relational video grammar: paraformant (2013, video, 6:27 mins.) featuring Nathan Evans
a relational video grammar: paragraph parameter (2012, video, 6:52 mins.) featuring Kate Pelling

As a participant in this project, the speech recorded during my 30 minute direct address to camera has been used both for this publication and for *a relational video grammar: paragraph parameter* (2012, video, 6:52 mins.). I felt that it was important to use self-generated speech for this publication because I did not want the transcription process to become a translation of another person's speech, as that would be an unnecessary extra element within the methodology. While this publication and *a relational video grammar: paragraph parameter* may share a common origin, they are not dependent on each other. In fact, there is no necessity to have seen any of the videos of *a relational video grammar* in order to appreciate what I am doing with this publication.

During the transcription of the 30 minutes of recorded material, sentences and paragraphs formed. These paragraphs provide the basic structure of this publication. The transcribed paragraphs are located on the left-hand pages. The text and drawings on the right-hand pages either refer directly to the transcription of speech located on the corresponding left-hand page; or refer to the process of making direct address to camera; or drive a narrative within the publication as a whole. Here, I am using Roland Barthes' idea that narrative is "a prodigious variety of genres" (1977, p.79) referring to the multiple layers of information within the pages of this publication, and the narrative possibilities within these layers. Constructing the publication in this way, allowed me to engage on many levels with linguistic and technological editing processes, without the necessity of using the format of video beyond the recording of the speech.

My use of 'grammar' in the title of this publication refers to the set of structural rules that govern the composition of speech. I am also making reference to 'grammar' as commonly used in relation to the language of mainstream film (Metz, 1974), and in turn artists' film and video, where there are many histories that situate the genre in relation to the birth of mainstream film, but also of having formed from disciplines such as painting and drawing (Rees, 1999). Whatever the origin of the genre, the technological editing tools available to artists' film and video share a similar grammar to that of mainstream film, although these structural rules may be adhered to, or resisted, in a number of different ways. Drawing plays an important role in *a relational video grammar*, and this in part acknowledges the alternative histories of artists' film and video, as well as providing a further tool for editing and interrogating the problematics within direct address to camera.

To explore the conceptual relationships between the linguistic and technological editing processes in direct address to camera, I have employed a number of methodologies. One method has been to apply multiple processes to a specific speech event, such as when the incorrect word is used in a sentence. Page 16 of this publication provides an example of this. During the direct address to camera I said "editing this document" and having said it, I realised that "document" was not the right word to use in the context of what I was trying to communicate. I acknowledged my mistake by employing one of the linguistic editing processes available to me, I said "Document is not the right word". Linguistic self-editing is largely an internal process, although in the case of self-listening there is a kind of "acoustic mirror" (Dolar 2006, p.40) where the individual hears and acknowledges their mistake, rather than catching and correcting the mistake before it is uttered. Technological solutions to the example of an incorrect word in the sentence, might be to use the video editing process to cut it out, to apply the correct word over the top of it using audio-dubbing, or to add the corrected word in subtitle text. For this publication, as video is not the ultimate result of the direct address to camera, then following the transcription of the speech, further text-based editing processes could be used, the incorrect word might be crossed out, erased, or the correct word could be added to the text. Page 16 in this publication shows the error as linguistically corrected at the point that the speech was generated, and then on page 17, it is highlighted and expanded on in the technological editing process.

The experimental nature of this publication resides in it being an extrapolation of the video editing process. 'Extrapolation' implies a sense of the unknown, where the definition of extrapolation is "to extend the application of (a method or conclusion) to an unknown situation by assuming that existing trends will continue or similar methods will be applicable" (Oxford English Dictionary, 2013). The application of this extrapolation was not towards a pre-determined conclusion, but an extension of the editing process beyond the format of video, to see what could be achieved. One of the unexpected results of putting together this publication has been that the transcribed speech and the edited version of the transcribed speech, appear on facing pages and actually touch each other prior to the publication being opened. This creates a physical relationship between the versions of edited material, that illustrates the conceptual relationship between self-editing prior to speech, and the post-recording technological editing process that I have been exploring.

This introduction can only be a brief guide to my area of interest, to give you an idea of how this publication came about. I am not so generous as to also provide conclusions at the end. This is an ongoing experiment and I am not yet ready to draw concrete conclusions, if indeed there are such a thing. This publication will have succeeded if you find yourself reflecting on the conceptual relationships that connect linguistic and technological editing processes, and particularly the selection, rejection, reconfiguration and obliteration of speech or text. However, I hope that you will also find enough space within these pages to think about the work based on your own points of reference. Ultimately, whatever this publication does provoke for you, I hope that it will be something meaningful.

References:

Barthes, R., 1977. *Image Music Text*. London: Fontana Press.

Dolar, M., 2006. *A Voice and Nothing More*. Cambridge, MA: Massachusetts Institute of Technology.

Metz, C., 1968. *Film Language: A Semiotics of the Cinema*. Translated from French by M. Taylor, 1974. New York: Oxford University Press.

Rees, A.L., 1999. *A History of Experimental Film and Video*. London: British Film Institute.

transcription | extrapolation

<<Switch Camera On and Set Timer>>

00:00:45 So, I am meant to be talking about talking to myself, or language and culture, or a subject I'm really interested in, or careful descriptions of things. That's the parameters of this experiment. My most useful subject for people to talk about in this situation is talking to themselves, because it's the most closely related to the actual process that is being undergone, most closely related to this actual situation. I am conducting this experiment as well as appearing in it, because I think it's important for me to have a presence within it, but also have a presence that's engaged with the process directly, I have experienced this process and that's important for me to have done that so that I can reassure the other participants as to exactly what is entailed in the process, in what they're doing.

This is a story about editing. It starts when Kate Pelling starts speaking, and the story ends when the bell rings and the speaking stops. In this case, the person speaking also happens to be the editor of the speech. This the the editor editing. Editing during the generation of the speech and also returning to the transcribed speech material afterwards in a technological editing process of some description. The editor needs to edit, as the editing process helps to understand and develop relationships with histories, processes, spaces and other people.

*RECORDING TOOK PLACE 19/08/2012 IN ELEPHANT+CASTLE, LONDON, UK

<<Switch Camera On and Set Timer>> [00:00:00]*

*KATE PELLING SAID:

00:00:45 So, I am meant to be talking about talking to myself, or language and culture, or a subject I'm really interested in, or careful descriptions of things. That's the parameters of this experiment. My most useful subject for people to talk about in this situation is talking to themselves, because it's the most closely related to the actual process that is being undergone, most closely related to this actual situation. I am conducting this experiment as well as appearing in it, because I think it's important for me to have a presence within it, but also have a presence that's engaged with the process directly, I have experienced this process and that's important for me to have done that so that I can reassure the other participants as to exactly what is entailed in the process, in what they're doing.

00:02:33 My overall area of interest is direct address to camera. I'm talking directly to the camera, using this microphone to capture the speech. Microphone's on. And I will be editing this afterwards; I'm editing this while I'm speaking, because I'm thinking about the speech, before it comes out of my mouth, before I release the speech, I'm thinking about what to say, and then I will be editing the video afterwards. In the participant's case, other participant's case, the process is slightly different in that I will be editing their speech. So, they edit their speech at the point of delivery, the point of release, and then I edit their speech afterwards. So it's still a double editing process, but performed by another, in their case. In this case it is performed by the same person – me.

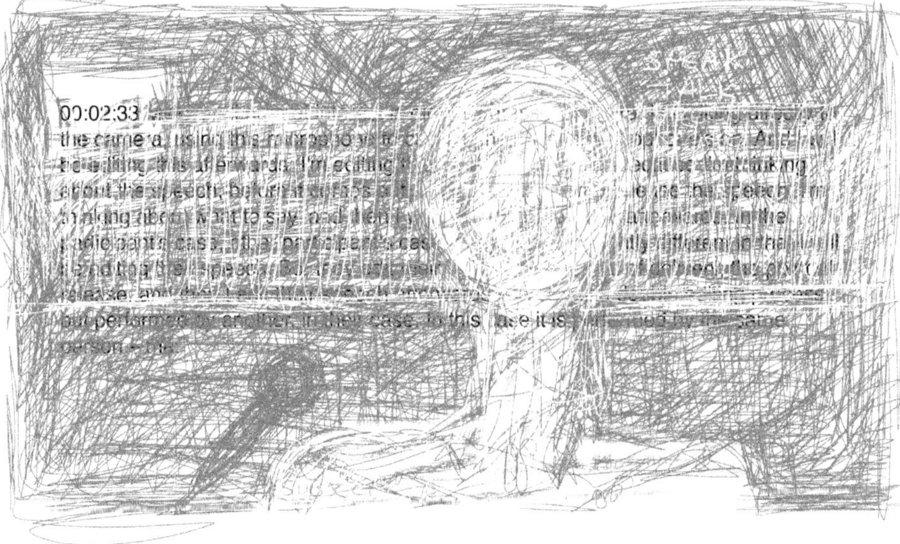
00:02:33

00:03:49 This process is part of a larger research project on editing speech within artist direct address to camera. It makes up a small part of a large project. So if I were to talk about talking to myself, I would say that I talk to myself a lot, I talk to a camera a lot, and I'm looking at myself in the monitor of the camera. I talk to myself in many different ways. I mutter to myself, I externalise thoughts, think through them to myself, I will provide commentary on various things to the room. And in this case I am talking to the camera as if it were a person not necessarily a future audience, but to myself as the future audience while I edit this. It's not actual audience, because I will be watching it, but I'm watching it with an editor's eye, so I'm watching it, looking at it, taking different consideration of what's being said, not watching it purely as an audience would. Because I'm making decisions about what I cut out and what I keep in, and what I'm going to do with the rest of it. So when I'm watching it later, as an editor, another editor, a mainstream film editor, described watching it back as a "substitute" audience; not a proper audience but a substitute audience. So I'm effectively talking to myself in the future, who will be watching this back and making those decisions. Decisions. I am keen to make that distinction, because me in the future watching it, and unknown future public watching this for any other future person watching this, because I think it's different it's a different case where I have a I have set up this process and I am going to be removing, editing out, large sections of it for the point of creating something that is then available to an audience. Possibly. That is a distinct activity from the then future audience person who might watch this. And that is necessary that I make that distinction.

[00:03:49] This process of editing a text document, object on editing speech within artists direct address to camera. It requires me to talk to myself and simultaneously talk directly to the camera, talking to a piece of technology with no mediation of another person. It is a process of editing in the generation of speech, editing before the speech reaches the camera.

myse ... vide commentary ...

am talking to the camera ...

... I edit this. ...

will h... Obliteration an editor's eye state of affairs.

at it. ...

audience enforcing a process of obliteration decisions ... before I cut out and what I keep in an editing process, and also to the text after it has been transcribed, where I am editor, another editor speech. ... editor, described ...

... not a pr... but a sublime audience.

The editing process is made up of a series of decisions to be made relating to the ... decisions. Decisions. Decisions to make ...

fu... watching it ... public wa...

person watching ... use I think ... it's ... a

I have set up this ... removing, editing out, ... ions

of it for the ... then ava... audience.

00:07:28 I am talking to myself, yes I am talking to myself, I am talking to myself in the present, I am talking to myself in the little monitor image. I am talking to myself in the future, where I am going to be editing this document. Document is not the right word. Editing this filming, that's not the right word either. Editing this material. Material is the right word.

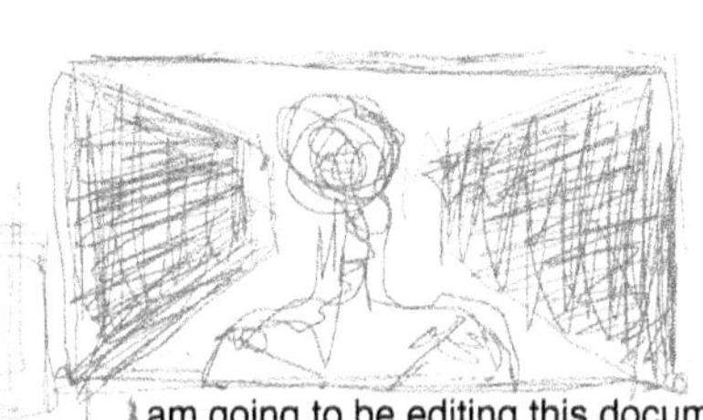

I am going to be editing this document. Document is not the right word. Editing this filming, that's not the right word either. Editing this material. Material is the right word.

I am going to be editing this document. Document is not the right word. Editing this filming, that's not the right word either. Editing this material. Material is the right word. I am going to be editing this document. Document is not the right word. Editing this filming, that's not the right word either. Editing this material. Material is the right word. I am going to be editing this document. Document is not the right word. Editing this filming, that's not the right word either. Editing the material. Material is the right word. I am going to be editing this document. Document is not the right word. Editing this filming, that's not the right word either.

00:08:01 Generated material. I'm talking myself in the present, where I am talking to a small image of myself in a monitor, that is attached to the camera. I am talking to myself in the future, the future person, me, who will be editing this material. I'm talking to an inanimate object, the camera, I'm getting no feedback from it, so I am just required to talk. And I am talking to myself, because I am, as I speak, I can listen, and I hear myself. So if I make a mistake, I can correct myself in the present, rather than having to read it back. Read it back? Watch it back, on the material that is generated by video in the editing process. I can correct myself as I go along through a speech-editing process.

00:08:01 Generated material. I'm talking myself in the present, where I am talking to a small image of myself in a monitor, that is attached to the camera. I am talking to myself in the future, the future person, me, who will be editing this material. I'm talking to an inanimate object, the camera, I'm getting no feedback from it, so I am just required to talk. And I am talking to myself, because I am, as I speak, I can listen, and I hear myself. So if I make a mistake, I can correct myself in the present, rather than having to read it back. Read it back? Watch it back, on the material that is generated by video in the editing process. I can correct myself as I go along through a speech-editing process.

EDITING IS NOT ABOUT CORRECTION THOUGH. THAT IMPLIES A VALUE SYSTEM OF GOOD/BAD WHICH IS AN OVER-SIMPLIFICATION OF THE DECISION-MAKING PROCESS. THE SELECT/REJECT/RECONFIGURE MODEL IS ON PHILOSOPHICALLY UNCERTAIN GROUNDS. HOWEVER TECHNICAL PROCESSES DO REQUIRE THIS OVERSIMPLIFICATION.

00:09:05 So, I am listening to myself in the present. I am talking to myself in the present and I am talking to myself int he future, and I am personifying the camera, and talking to that at the same time. There are four strands going on there in one process. There's probably more, but that's where I'm up to.

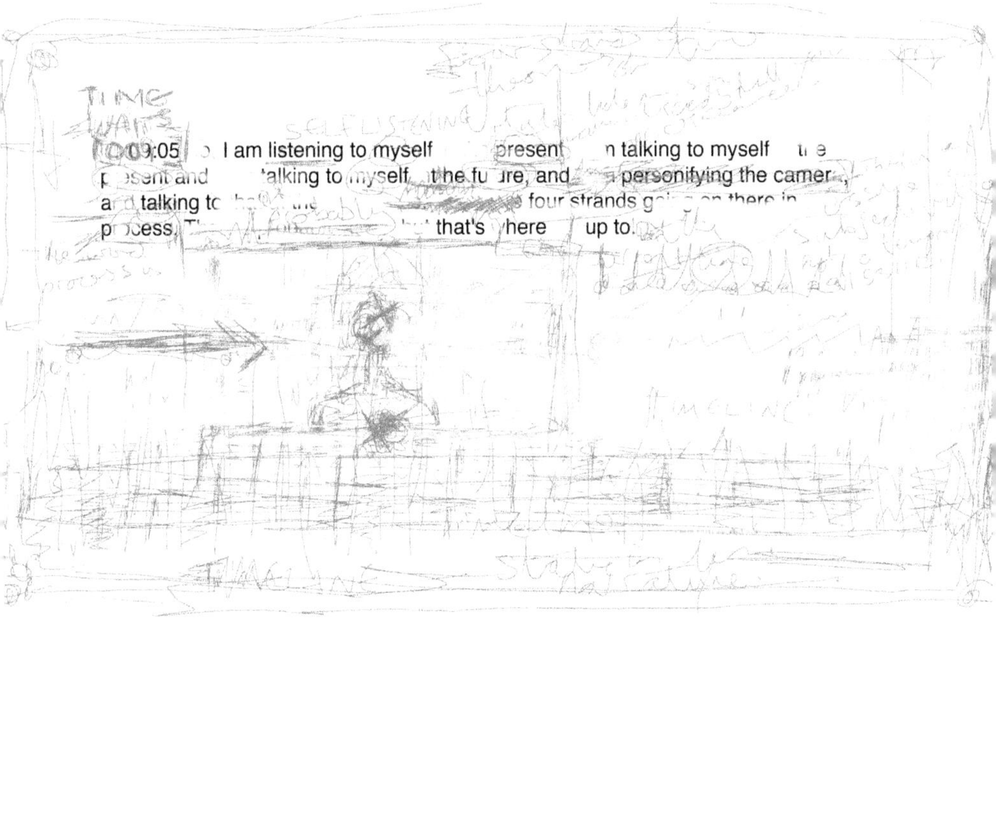

09:05 [illegible] I am listening to myself [illegible] present [illegible]n talking to myself [illegible] present and [illegible] talking to myself [illegible] the future, and [illegible] personifying the camera, and talking to [illegible] four strands go[illegible] on there in process. [illegible] that's [illegible]here [illegible] up to.

00:09:38 The process of generating speech, when you're talking to yourself, is the same to a camera as when you're talking to yourself and there's no camera there. You just speak. There is a self-consciousness attached to the camera being there because there's a sense of permanency, there's actual permanency about it. It's being recorded. But that permanency is also up to me, whether I release the edited material or not. Which often I don't. Often it doesn't get that far.

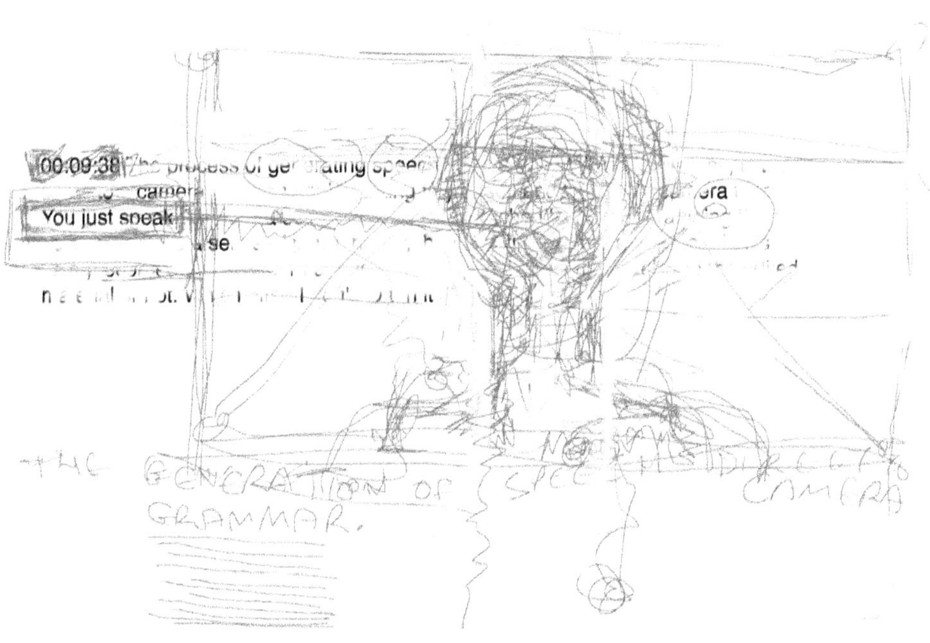
00:09:38
You just speak
GRAMMAR.

00:10:27 So the process is the same, you generate speech in the same way, you consider what you're going to say and you say it. You might not be very careful about what you say because there's nobody listening, because you're on your own, because you might be able to edit it out later anyway. So it doesn't matter if you make mistakes, if you can't think of what word to use, it doesn't matter if you talk nonsense, complete nonsense, because that can be edited out afterwards in the technological editing process. In the same way that talking to yourself when there's nobody present, no camera present, you can talk absolute nonsense, you can make mistakes, you can say whatever you like because nobody's listening. Nobody's recording, nobody's listening.

[00:10:27] [INCORRECT] , you generate speech [INCORRECT] . you consider what you're going to say and you say it. You might not be very careful about what you say '[INCORRECT], [INCORRECT] [INCORRECT,] [INCORRECT] you might be able to edit it out later anyway. [IN] it doesn't matter if you make mistakes, if you can't think of what word to use, [INCORRECT] [INCORRECT] [INCORRECT], [INCORRECT] ... that can be edited out afterwards in the technological editing process. [INCORRECT] talking to yourself when there's nobody present, no camera present, you can talk [INCORRECT] you can make mistakes, you can say whatever you like '[INCORRECT]. [INCORRECT] [INCORRECT], [INCORRECT] [INCORRECT] that when there is a camera present, when you are talking to a recording camera rather than just to yourself, you do not talk nonsense because it is recording, it is different to talking to yourself. This process has more in common with writing in a personal diary (without the personal information) [INCORRECT] the process of writing means that the words are carefully considered, but there is a specific purpose to the exercise, which negates the talking of rubbish, but the audience is intended to be only yourself. It's a complicated combination of relationships, between yourself and the camera, yourself and yourself, and yourself and the potential future audience. [INCORRECT]

00:11:18 So that's a pretty big difference. The difference in the process has to do with the permanency of it, it has to do with the focus of the camera, and the way it doesn't move. But you know it's recording. It's an incredible scrutiny that you go through sitting in front of it, because I know that this is HD video, it can pick up every single hair on your head, if I wasn't wearing a wig.

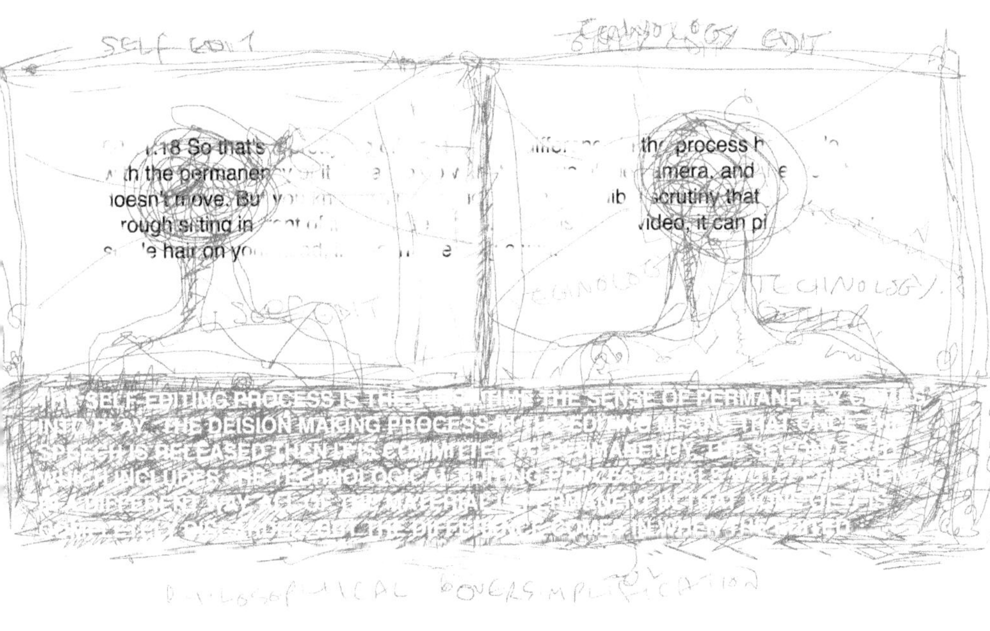
SELF EDIT
TECHNOLOGY EDIT
.18 So that's
th the permanen
amera, and
oesn't move. Bu
scrutiny that
rough sitting in
video, it can p
hair on yo
TECHNOLOGY
SELF EDITING PROCESS IS THE
THE SENSE OF PERMANENCY
INTO PLAY. THE DEISION MAKING PROCESS
SPEECH IS RELEASED THEN IT IS COMMITTED TO PERMANENCY.
WHICH INCLUDES THE TECHNOLOGICAL EDITING PROCESS
DIFFERENT WAY
MATERIAL IS PERMANENT IN THAT NONE OF IT IS
BUT THE DIFFERENCE COMES IN WHEN
PHILOSOPHICAL OVERSIMPLIFICATION

00:12:13 Scrutiny, that's it. I was hoping that I'd run out of things to say at some point. I need to do this process more often, so I don't have so much to say, I think it's more valuable the spaces and thinking, than just, just speech, constant constant speech.

00:12:13 Scrutiny, that's it. I was hoping that I'd run out of things to say at some point. I need to do this process more often, so I don't have so much to say, I think it's more valuable the spaces and thinking, than just, just speech, constant constant speech.

00:13:24 I have a timer in place, to make sure that I don't exceed half an hour, or fall short of half an hour, because after years of experimenting I have discovered that half an hour is the optimum time length to ask somebody to do this, it's not excessively long where it becomes stressful, and at the same time it's not so short that I don't get anything any material to work with. So half an hour it is. I'm applying the same rules to myself, I've got a timer, and I've set it for half an hour, and I will talk, and do the direct address the camera for the full half an hour.

00:13:24 I have a timer in place, to make sure that I don't exceed half an hour, or fall short of half an hour, because after years of experimenting I have discovered that half an hour is the optimum time length to ask somebody to do this, it's not excessively long where it becomes stressful, and at the same time it's not so short that I don't get anything any material to work with. So half an hour it is. I'm applying the same rules to myself, I've got a timer, and I've set it for half an hour, and I will talk, and do the direct address the camera for the full half an hour.

00:14:24 I will talk about talking to myself. I will talk about making speech, I will talk about generating speech. All the things I have asked everybody else to talk about (whether they have or not is different).

THINK ABOUT MAKING SPEECH
THINK ABOUT GENERATING SPEECH

00:14:24 I will talk about talking to myself. I will talk about making speech, I will talk about generating speech. All the things I have asked everybody else to talk about.

Nathan Evans
Otelo M Fabião
James Graham-Campbell
Tzvet Lazar
Michael Twaits

THIS REFERS TO THE PROCESS OF MAKING THE VIDEOS IN A RELATIONAL VIDEO GRAMMAR. ALL PARTICIPANTS WERE ASKED TO TALK DIRECTLY TO THE CAMERA FOR A 30 MINUTE SESSION; THEY WERE LEFT ALONE WITH THE CAMERA. I AS THE EDITOR THEN EDIT THE VIDEO. I ALSO DID RECORDING DIRECT TO CAMERA.

00:14:36 The process is set in place, and whether people follow it or not is up to them. There is no right or wrong in this process it is about generating speech. Editing speech in front of the camera, so that it can be edited, and then it can be edited afterwards, and exploring that process to see what I can discover about speech and the generation of speech in front of the camera.

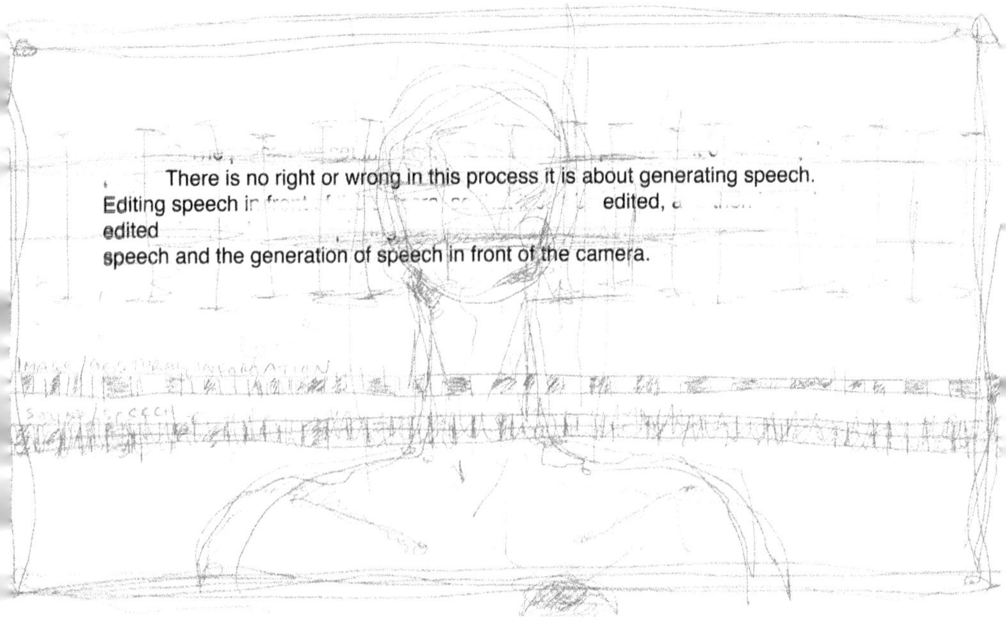

There is no right or wrong in this process it is about generating speech. Editing speech in [illegible] edited, [illegible] edited

speech and the generation of speech in front of the camera.

00:15:08 Prof John Sturgeon has offered to show me how to make a poor man's Interrotron, I'm going to look forward to that, that's Errol Morris' Interrotron that I'm referring to. The generation of speech. I'm finding it hard to make eye contact with the camera today because I've got the lights in front of the camera, and the lights are each side, and the camera in between is actually quite… with it being behind the lights, I forget what the word is, it's in shadow, but it's more than that, it's… I don't know. I don't know what the word is. I don't know what the word is. Chiaroscuro is a good word, but it's not that word. Light and dark.

CAMERA LIVE FEED
MONITOR
WHERE EYELINE = AS CLOSE AS POSSIBLE TO CAMERA DIRECTLY.

00.15.08 IT'S QUITE NORMAL TO REFERENCE RECENT CONVERSATIONS YOU MAY HAVE HAD WHILE TALKING TO A CAMERA. I'M INTERESTED IN The generation of speech. AND THIS IS ABOUT NATURAL SPEECH camera AND THE SUBSEQUENT EDITING THAT OCCURS DURING THE camera, PROCESS OF DIRECT ADDRESS TO CAMERA. BUILDING A GRAMMAR, I forget what the word is, WHERE GRAMMAR INCLUDES ELEMENTS OF I don't know. I don't know what the word is, I do... LANGUAGE IN TERMS OF good word, but it's not that word. SPEECH AND OF VIDEO AND TEXT. TALKING, OR WRITING, ABOUT VIDEO WITHOUT USING VIDEO IS QUITE LIBERATING - ALTHOUGH THE VIDEO IS PRESENT, BUT IN THE PAST, AS THE SPEECH OCCURRED IN THE PAST, A TRANSCRIPTION PROCESS TOOK PLACE AND THEN THE TRANSCRIPTION MATERIAL IS EDITED, THAT IS THE PRESENT AS I AM WRITING THIS.

00:17:20 It's okay to stop talking, I can pause, I don't have to talk for a full half an hour. It would be quite difficult to do that actually.

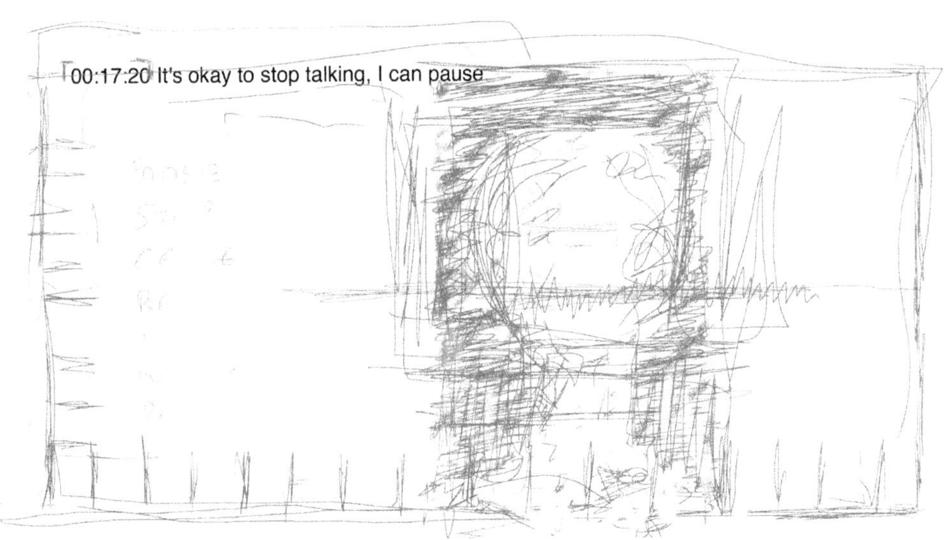

00:17:20 It's okay to stop talking, I can pause

00:17:44 I'll see what time I've got left.

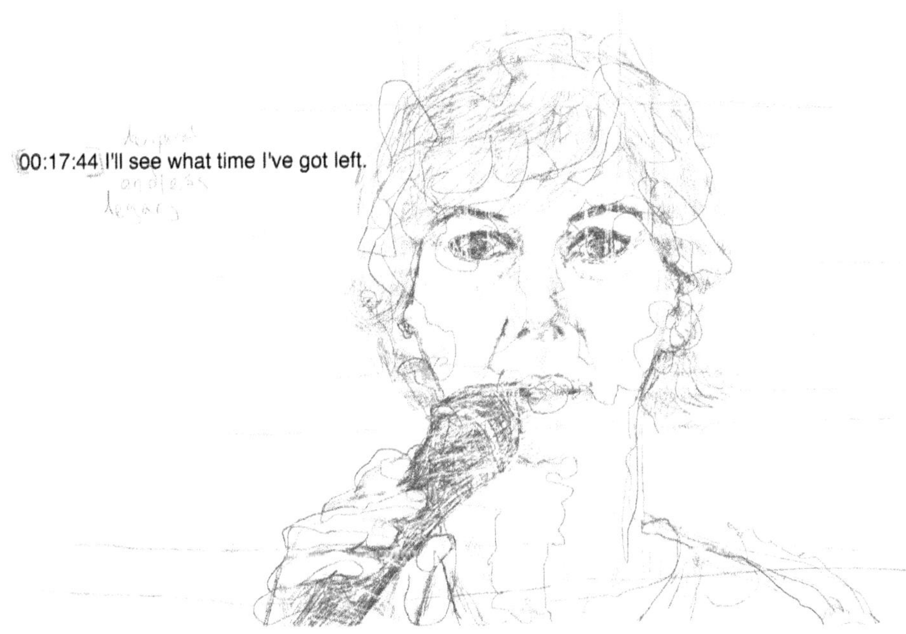

00:17:44 I'll see what time I've got left.

00:17:51 Actually I've only got eleven minutes left. So I've already done twenty minutes. It must have taken twenty minutes to exhaust everything I wanted to say and now I'm left at the really interesting bit where I have to actually think of what to say, as I'm saying it. Instead of all the things that I'd built up in my mind that I wanted to talk about, that's now cleared, and I've got to a stage of the process where I am generating speech purely, improvised speech, although I don't use the word improvised, I mean purely, fresh speech. Improvisation is not the word. It's fresh, fresh speech that I haven't already mulled over my head once. I wasn't thinking about it this morning when I knew I was doing filming later. I'm now at the point where I can speak directly to the camera with speech that hasn't been thought through., I suppose. I think it through in that I'm editing as I'm speaking, and that's why I'm speaking in sentences, or near enough. I am speaking in series of words that make sense because I'm using the resource of my whole life's worth of learning language, and I'm using that body of knowledge in order to generate language. But editing it as I speak, I'm looking for speech errors, I'm looking for mistakes, I'm looking for elements where I may not have actually conveyed meaning as intended. So usually you would look at the other person's face when you're talking to them, and you would notice by their facial expression that they haven't understood quite what you were saying, or that they'd misunderstood what you were saying. You would be able to redeliver the sentence, or the utterance, with different emphasis, in a different way, using different words, in order to get your meaning across to the person. Whether then they still misunderstand, you end up in a cyclical situation, until they understand.

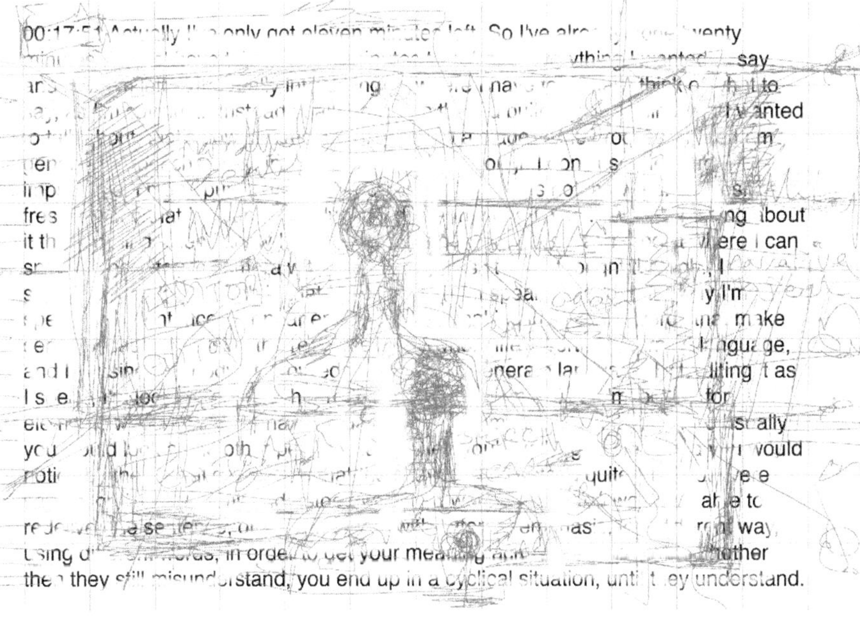

00:20:33 The camera doesn't do that, the camera doesn't react, it doesn't reflect anything that I'm saying. So it's up to me as a self-listener to look out for speech errors. If I say a word wrong, if I say a word that doesn't come out properly, or I say a word that is the wrong word to use, then I can pick up on that, because I just heard what I've just said, and I can repeat it either correctly, or I can use a different word, or I can quantify that it was a different word by saying "I didn't mean that", or "that's the wrong word", and then I can use the right word in order to correct myself. When I'm editing, I'm not looking for perfect speech, I'm not looking for narrative structure. I'm looking for ways of exposing the generation of language. So whereas this process of me talking to camera is all about ordering the speech into a sense that, into a... not a 'sense', ordering the speech into an order? It's about ordering the speech, so that it could be understood within normal English-language grammatical sense, and structure.

00:00:22 The camera doesn't do that, the camera doesn't react, it doesn't reflect
any [illegible] speech
erro[illegible] y, [illegible] I say a
wo[illegible] heard
wha[illegible] word, or
I ca[illegible] 's the
wro[illegible] I'm
edi[illegible]. I'm
loo[illegible] ess of
me[illegible] ... not a
'se[illegible] ech, so that it
could be understood within normal English-language grammatical sense, and
structure.

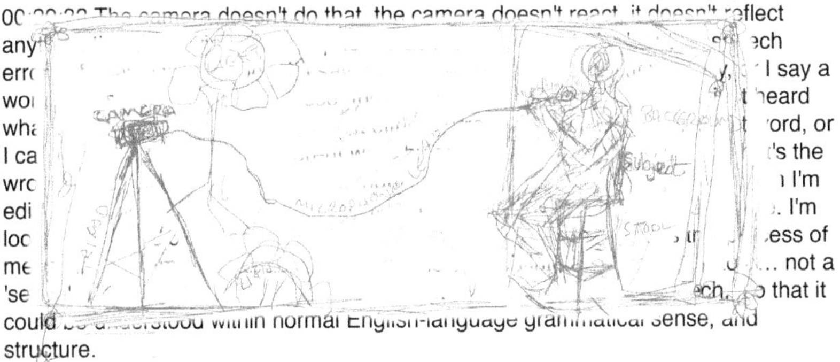

00:22:14 I could talk nonsense, but that doesn't make sense in terms of editing afterwards. If I edit the sense out of the speech afterwards because I'm interested in editing, seeing what I can do to the speech in the editing process, and I'm not concerned with narrative. But if I started with something that doesn't have a sentence form, it doesn't have grammatical structure, or any interesting errors that have been corrected, then I haven't got anything to start with. I could speak rubbish, I could say completely uninteresting things, but that's going to make it a very dull edit, and pointless.

00:22:14 I could talk nonsense, but that doesn't make sense in terms of editing afterwards. If I edit the sense out of the speech afterwards because I'm interested in editing, seeing what I can do to the speech in the editing process, and I'm not concerned with narrative. But if I started with something that doesn't have a sentence form, it doesn't have grammatical structure, or any interesting errors that have been corrected, then I haven't got anything to start with. I could speak rubbish, I could say completely uninteresting things, but that's going to make it a very dull edit, and pointless.

00:22:14 I could talk nonsense, but that doesn't make sense in terms of editing afterwards. If I edit the sense out of the speech afterwards because I'm interested in editing, seeing what I can do to the speech in the editing process, and I'm not concerned with narrative. But if I started with something that doesn't have a sentence form, it doesn't have grammatical structure, or any interesting errors that have been corrected, then I haven't got anything to start with. I could speak rubbish, I could say completely uninteresting things, but that's going to make it a very dull edit, and pointless.

my uncle billy had a ten foot willy and he showed it to the girl next door. she thought it was a snake, and hit it with a rake, and now it's only six foot four.

00:23:08 Because what's the point in undoing something that is already undone, I suppose is what I'm saying, I think. So grammar and speech has to be quite rigid, the way we generate it has to be quite rigid because it lays a firm foundation for what then the process continues, where I can then undo it and examine it. Because I have to undo it to examine it. But I have to also acknowledge that if I undid it at this process, the generation of the speech process, then the experiment stops there. It is not about the relationship between editing speech in my mind as I generate speech, and editing video in the technological editing process afterwards. In that scenario, there is only one edit, and it is not within my remit of this project. Hopefully that makes sense.

[00:23:08] B[PAUSE]hat's [PAUSE] undoing [PAUSE] that is already undone, I s[PAUSE] what I'm saying [PAUSE] So grammar and speech has to be quite [PAUSE] th[PAUSE] generate it has to be quite [PAUSE] ecause it lays a firm f[PAUSE] or what then the process [PAUSE] where I can then undo it and examine it. ~~Because I have~~ to undo it to examine it. B[PAUSE] also acknowledge that if I undid it at this [PAUSE] p[PAUSE] he generation of the speech process, then the experiment stops there. It is [PAUSE] the relationship between editing speech in [PAUSE] I generate speech, and editing video in the technological editing process [PAUSE]. In that scenario, there is only one edit, and it is [PAUSE] remit of [PAUSE]. Hopefully that makes sense. [STOP AND THINK ABOUT THIS]

00:24:30 I've only got five minutes left. I don't want to be in full flow when the time runs out. Because I could be, I've done an hour of this many, many, many, many times. and I could easily be in full flow at the point of half an hour.

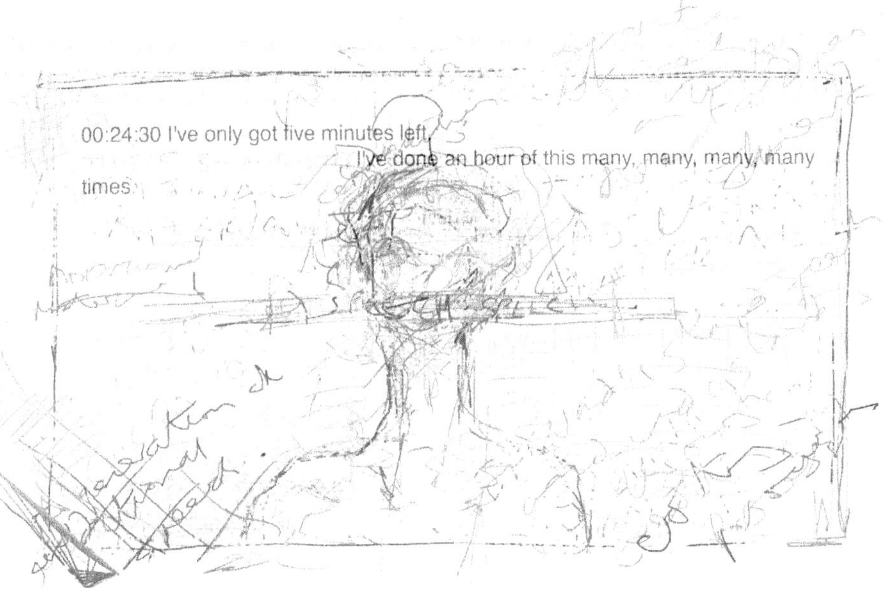
00:24:30 I've only got five minutes left.
I've done an hour of this many, many, many, many times.

00:24:50 Anything else I need to add into this? At this stage. Why am I wearing a wig? I need the light to reflect off me. I'm in front of a camera. There's all ousts of things that could answer that question. There's two of many reasons. Prosthesis. I need prosthesis, and additional material for myself, for my sense of self-consciousness. In order to minimise self-consciousness I suppose. Or to support my self-consciousness. I'm using 'self-conscious' in two different ways there.

00:24:50 Anything else I need to add into this? ~~At this stage.~~ Why am I wearing a wig? I need the light to reflect off me. I'm in front of a camera. There's all ~~sorts~~ of things that could answer that question. There's two of many reasons. Prosthesis. I need prosthesis, and additional material for myself, for my sense of self-consciousness. In order to minimise self-consciousness ~~I suppose. Or to support~~ my self-consciousness. I'm using 'self-conscious' in two different ways there.

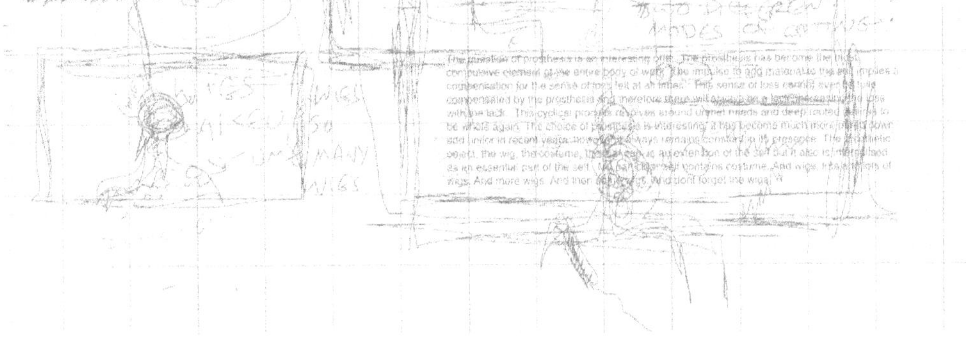

The question of prosthesis is an interesting one. The prosthesis has become the most compulsive element of the entire body of work. The impulse to add material to the self implies a compensation for the sense of loss felt at all times. This sense of loss cannot ever be fully compensated by the prosthesis and therefore there will always be a lack [illegible] the loss with the lack. This cyclical process revolves around unmet needs and deep rooted desires to be whole again. The choice of prosthesis is interesting; it has become much more pared down and uniform in recent years, however it always remains constant in its presence. The prosthetic object, the wig, the costume, these can act as an extension of the self but it also is internalised as an essential part of the self. My [illegible] contains costume. And wigs. Lots and lots of wigs. And more wigs. And then [illegible] wigs. And don't forget the wigs.

00:25:56 That could get really complicated. That's a whole different video. I have generated a lot of speech, and this is going to be quite difficult, I'm going to be transcribing this. I don't like transcribing speech it is the worst, worst point of this entire process, but it has to be done. And that's another reason for only doing half an hour and not an hour, because of the sheer volume of transcription work that I have to do over the next few months.

00:25:56 That could get really complicated. That's a whole different video. I have generated a lot of speech, and this is going to be quite difficult. I'm going to be transcribing this. ~~I don't like transcribing speech it is the worst, worst point of this entire process, but it has to be done. And that's another reason for only doing half an hour and not an hour, because of the sheer volume of transcription work that I have to do over the next few months.~~

00:26:37 At least then I get to do the fun bit which is editing the transcriptions, as well as the fun bit of editing the actual video. I edit the text as well as the video. It seems that I am approaching every area of this I possibly could, although I'm open to suggestions, if there's any area that I might have missed.

EDIT TEXT

00:26:37 At least then I get to do the fun bit which is editing the transcriptions, as well as the fun bit of editing the actual video. I edit the text as well as the video

EDIT VIDEO

EDITOR EDITS

EDITOR'S EDIT

00:27:05 Because, I'm thorough and I want to understand this process, and I want to really mine it to gain everything I possibly can out of understanding this process. And using the editing process as a tool for understanding the generation of speech in front of a camera in artists' film and video. That feels like a very final point to end on, but of course the time doesn't run out at that point, I've still got two minutes.

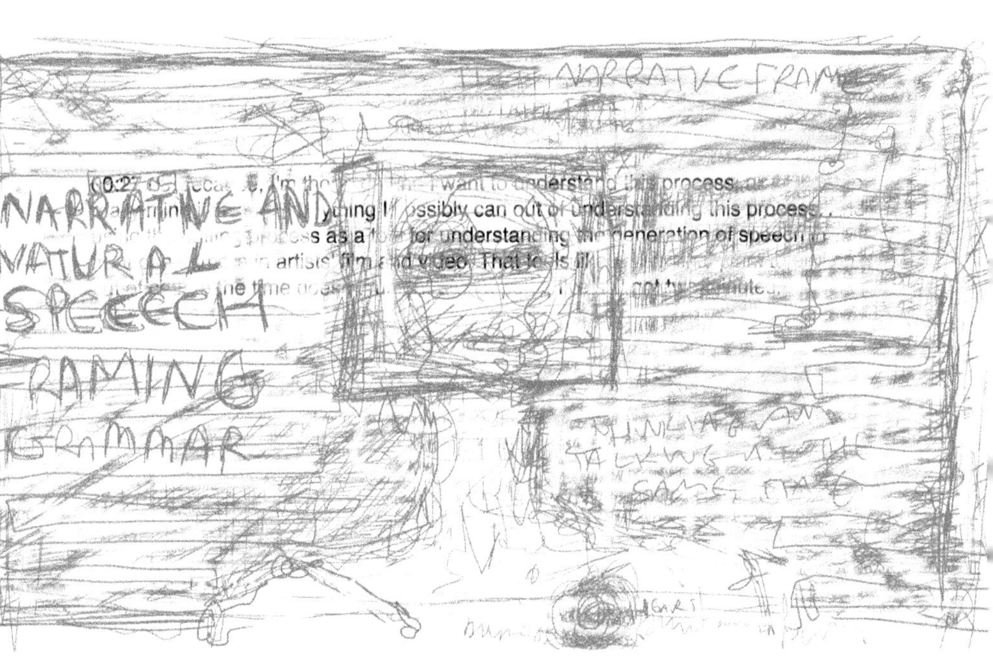
NARRATIVE FRAME
NARRATIVE AND
NATURAL
SPEECH
FRAMING
GRAMMAR
ything I possibly can out of understanding this process
s as a tool for understanding the generation of speech in
in artists' film and video. That feels like

00:27:40 So I've gone "ta-dahhhhh" , I've said a really amazing thing to end on, well, not that amazing, but a good ending point anyway, and of course I've still got two minutes. So I might look at the camera for two minutes. I could easily look at the camera for half an hour, but I wouldn't do that to myself, because I'm generating speech and I need something to work with. That's the basic idea of it. And this is artists' film and video, I can do anything in front of the camera, and edit it in any way I choose. Although there must be some parameters. WIthin an experiment, as long as it supports my experiment, I suppose there are parameters to this. I am supporting my experiment by investing in this process, by going through this process myself, and asking these other people to go through the process as well.

00:27:40 "ta-dahhhhh" , I've said a really amazing thing to end on, not that amazing, but a good ending point anyway,

camera I'm generating speech

artists' film and video

choose. Although there must be some parameters. Within an experiment, I suppose there are parameters to this.

my experiment

00:29:12 There's like less than a minute on the clock now. I'll just wait for that to go off.

<<Bell Rings and Camera is Switched Off>>

00:29:12 There's like less than a minute on the clock now. I'll just wait for that to go off.

<<Bell Rings and Camera is Switched Off>>

and she learnt that everything is edited. even real life. But in real life the camera is never switched off, and you are duped into thinking that you can't edit anything when you can edit just about everything. apart from other people's work. you can't edit that. And* they all lived happily ever after.
*having made this realisation

The End

;)

biography

Kate Pelling is a UK based artist whose research-led practice consists of video, drawing and text. Kate Pelling studied at Wirral Metropolitan College, Birkenhead (2003), Wimbledon School of Art, London (2004), and Birkbeck, University of London (2008). She has exhibited extensively in the UK and the USA, and also in Bulgaria, Canada, Germany, Italy, Lithuania, Portugal, and Switzerland. Notable screenings include a retrospective at Shortini International Film Festival, Augusta, Italy, (2011) and *Talking To Myself In Public Again: A Screening of Video Works By Kate Pelling* at Chelsea College of Art & Design, London, UK (2012). Kate Pelling lives in London with a seraglio of handsome young men.

acknowledgements

I would like to thank Nathan Evans, Otelo M Fabião, James Graham-Campbell, Tzvet Lazar and Michael Twaits for their participation in the *a relational video grammar* experimental videos. I would also like to thank Dr Hayley Newman, Dr Linda Sandino and Jordan Baseman for their continuing support with my extended endeavour. A special thanks goes to Nathan Evans and Hazel Pelling for their endless support and encouragement. A few historical thanks are owed, for support given in the years leading up to this project – thank you to Prof. Oriana Baddeley, Prof. Catherine Elwes, Laura Lanceley, Dr Aaron McPeake, Dr Malcolm Quinn, Dr Paul Ryan and Prof. John Sturgeon. There are many others who have also helped me along the way, you are too numerous to name individually, but thank you anyway.

This publication is dedicated to the memory of my brothers, John and Stuart Pelling.

www.ingramcontent.com/pod-product-compliance
Ingram Content Group UK Ltd.
Pitfield, Milton Keynes, MK11 3LW, UK
UKHW020234250726
13967UKWH00001B/358